72 Golf Tips & Ins
Beginn

By Jeff Shaw

Introduction

I started playing golf ten years ago without any instruction, and to be honest I found the whole thing a little baffling. There were so many things I didn't understand that would have saved me countless strokes, but because I didn't know them I regularly failed to break 100, which frankly wasn't that enjoyable.

Things changed when I started playing with two friends who were already very good at golf (and extremely patient). One was a teaching professional at the club I joined who had an encyclopaedic knowledge of the swing and common amateur flaws, while the other played off a handicap of 3.5 and had a best round of 64 on the par 72 course. I started playing with them twice a week which as you can imagine became a test of patience for them and a test of coping with merciless ridicule for me. Eventually they realised that it was in their interests to help me get better and they began dropping in some very useful tips amongst the put downs.

I have shared the most valuable ones here in this book. We all know we should spend more time on the range or spend some money on lessons, but the truth is most of us just want to play at a level that makes the game enjoyable. The tips in this book are pretty much instant fixes that will work immediately without practice or time on the range.

These tips worked for me; they probably save me twenty shots a round on what I used to score. I have structured them into six sections so that they are easy to reference. The categories are: Long game, Short game, Putting, Course management, Mental game, and Common mistakes. Enjoy the tips and more importantly enjoy better golfing!

Long Game

The long game is the part of golf that probably got you hooked in the first place and will likely contain some of your most satisfying as well as soul destroying moments. My two friends could drive the ball well over 300 yards so I always felt intimidated and emasculated every time I teed it up with them. Trying to belt the ball as hard as I could didn't work out too well so eventually I decided to focus on technique and found the following tips a massive help. I still can't hit it as far as my friends but at least I don't look stupid anymore trying to match them.

Tip 1: Hitting it straight

When you absolutely have to hit the ball straight, try teeing the ball down slightly lower and feel like you are compressing the back of the golf ball into the ground as you strike. Shorten your finish like a punch shot.

Tip 2: Hitting it straight (part 2)

Imagine you are standing on the tee looking down a narrow fairway with a tight tree line on either side. You need to hit it straight or your second shot will be from the trees; but it's those trees that are making you nervous and will likely cause a bad tee shot. Here's the solution. Don't try aiming at a target two hundred yards away, instead imagine a hoop ten yards in front of you and try and hit the ball through that instead. It will feel like a much easier task allowing you to swing more confidently and the long distance target will take care of itself.

Tip 3: Gain the confidence to hit longer clubs

If you aren't used to hitting longer irons or woods they can sometimes feel very long, heavy, and unwieldy. To cancel this out try swinging something heavier like a broom, or two clubs held together. When you switch back to a lighter golf club it will feel like a feather and give you much more confidence and a feeling of control.

Tip 4: Gain the confidence to hit longer clubs (part 2)

To play longer clubs you are not confident in hitting try choking down the grip by half an inch. This is useful when you are progressing from say a 3 wood to a driver which may feel much longer. You can gain confidence by hitting the driver as if it was a 3 wood, simply by choking down the grip. The lower loft will ensure that the ball goes further and lower than it would have done with the 3 wood but you will still retain 3 wood control. This works on irons too. When you choke down on any iron, play the shot as though you are playing the next club down. For example if you are playing a choked down 5 iron, make sure your ball position and set up are as they would be for a 6 iron.

Tip 5: How to get more power on longer clubs

Longer clubs need club head speed to hit them well; but if you try and achieve this by swinging harder your swing mechanics will break down and your ball striking will decline. In order to strike cleanly and quickly through the ball try and imagine a second ball in front of the real one. Pretend the real one doesn't exist and focus on hitting the imaginary ball; you will connect with the real ball with much more power.

Tip 6: For added power start down slow

The key to striking the ball well with good timing and mechanics is the discipline of starting the downswing slowly. Never attack the ball from the top of the swing! You aren't going to add power like you think you will; instead you are going to break down the correct sequencing of your swing. This can lead to any manner of ball striking errors including the dreaded over the top movement which causes the weak slice of many amateurs. The swing should begin slowly and gather speed gradually up to the point of impact when the club-head should be at its fastest point. If you swing hard from the top your hands and arms may outrace your shoulders and body, meaning ironically the club-head is actually slowing down at impact, costing you power.

Tip 7: Keep swing tempo consistent

If you want to be a consistent hitter the swing tempo should be the same for every club in your bag. Too many players try to swing harder with longer clubs like the driver because they believe they have to in order to get the ball up in the air or achieve the extra distance. Attempting to use a different swing speed for each club will lead to inconsistent results. If you have ever walked off the course and said to your friend I was hitting the irons really well but couldn't hit the woods (or vice versa) that's a good indication you don't have a consistent swing speed. Trust in the inherent design of the clubs to give you the added distance and swing at the same speed.

Tip 8: Swing through the ball, don't hit at it.

How many people make a great looking practice swing, then address the ball and lash at it with a swing that looks nothing like the one they did ten seconds earlier? Too many golfers break down when you put a ball in front of them because they are consumed by the task of hitting the ball rather than making a good golf swing. Instead of thinking of the ball as a target, simply think of it as an object that gets in the way of the swing. You need to have the confidence that the swing will pick up the ball along the way otherwise you will be making all sorts of swing compensations to ensure you make contact. This is mentally hard to do so you might want to try it on the range first, but it's worth persevering with.

Tip 9: Ingrain your swing

People practice their swing without the ball all the time. They watch their backswing, hold position at the top and then look where the club is pointing; they look at the club at impact and then again after the follow through. However, when you swing for real you can't look at your club position because you should be intensely focused on the ball. You need to get the feel for your swing in each position. To accomplish this try swinging in very slow motion with your eyes closed. Your body will begin to recognise how each position feels making it like second nature.

Tip 10: Shake hands with the target

To promote straight shots with plenty of power remember to shake hands with the target after impact. Many amateurs struggle to get the clubface square at the point of impact leading to weak and high shots as the clubface glances the ball. To make sure you rotate your hands correctly imagine that your right hand is shaking hands with someone down the target line. If that still doesn't do it then try swinging the club above the ball so you can see how the hands should release at the point where the clubface hits the ball.

Tip 11: Always use a tee peg on a par 3

I have seen a number of people choose to hit their tee shot off the ground instead of a tee when using an iron. Air offers much less resistance than the ground, so make sure you always take the free advantage of using a tee peg and hit the ball under optimum conditions. Tiger Woods and Jack Nicklaus follow this advice, so you should too!

Tip 12: How to vary distance with one club

Most people are more comfortable hitting a full shot the maximum distance than a shorter "feel" shot. However there are times (usually when hitting into a green) that you need to hit a shorter shot, and this is where a lot of amateurs struggle. Let's imagine that you hit a full pitching wedge 120 yards, but you are faced with a shot into the green of 100 yards. Many amateurs use a back swing of similar length to their full swing and then in a desire to take power off the shot they decelerate into the ball. This usually causes a duff or a heavy shot that covers about a third of the distance you intended it to. The key to hitting shorter shots is to keep your swing speed and follow through exactly the same, but shorten your backswing! The shorter backswing will reliably reduce the power of your shot so that you can swing through confidently at full speed to a full finish. Now hitting short shots is a simple matter of shortening your backswing the appropriate amount.

Tip 13: Practice baseball for a natural swing

Every golfer strives for the perfect swing and at some point gets bogged down in the mechanics of their swing to the point where it no longer feels natural. If your swing feels like a series of jerky checkpoints rather than a fluid motion try this drill. Grip your club as if you were taking a normal swing, then raise the club in front of you so it is parallel to the ground. Now make a swing by turning your shoulders and hips as if you are swinging a baseball bat. This will give you the correct feeling of turning your body on the backswing and downswing. When that feels comfortable lower the club slightly so that it is two feet off the ground and repeat the exercise. Keep lowering the club face until the club is back in your normal address position. You should have the muscle memory of the baseball swing and should now be able to apply it to a real shot.

Tip 14: Alignment. It helps if you aim at the flag to start with!

Alignment is a crucial part of hitting your target, but the reality is it's very tough to aim when you are stood sideways on to the target as you are at address. My playing partners kept telling me I was aiming about twenty degrees to the left, but to me it felt like I was aiming dead online. Consequently my shots were yards off target. When my friends stood behind me and lined me up straight I felt like I was aiming twenty degrees to the right. Because I didn't trust what they were telling me I swung across to compensate, producing a slice. The fact is I couldn't trust my alignment because it felt uncomfortable when I was aligned with the target. To build trust that you are aligned try putting a club down on the ground pointing at the target. At address stand with your feet touching the club and you should find it doesn't feel so uncomfortable because you know for certain it must be online. Play a few practice rounds like this until you build a natural feel. Obviously you can't do this in competition so to avoid relapsing draw a mental line on the ground to help you align. Pick a divot or chunk of grass a yard in front of you that is on the target line and aim using that.

Tip 15: Set your swing speedo to 85%

The secret to consistent ball striking is to swing well within yourself. Tiger Woods says that on average he swings at about 85% of his full swing speed. He finds this gives him consistency and allows proper sequencing of his swing to take place. Slow your swing down instead of trying to hit the spots off it and you should notice much cleaner ball striking and no loss in distance (because the strike is most important in determining distance). Now this is the really important bit. Once you have mastered this and got a swing with a great ball strike, the temptation is to stand on the tee looking at the wide open fairway thinking "wow my swing is great, if I swing just a tiny bit harder I will be hitting this ball miles"! As soon as you give into the voices in your head your ball striking and consistency will fall away again.

Short Game

Let's be realistic, learning the short game is nowhere near as much fun as being able to belt the ball miles. But please please please don't dismiss this section; it has a far greater influence on your score than the previous section.

Tip 16: Don't duff your chips

Many amateurs play a chip shot with a long backswing, and then fearful of over hitting they decelerate into the ball. Ironically this makes it more likely that you will thin it long over the green or even duff it half way. Instead, play a compact backswing which is low to the ground and then hit through the ball with speed, and with your head down. A clean strike will go further than you think.

Tip 17: Don't duff your chips (part 2)

The number one mistake amateurs make when chipping is trying to flip their wrists through impact. This probably happens because the person doesn't trust the clubface to get the ball in the air and they feel like it needs a little help. Remember the club will do the work for you! Always start the chip with your hands ahead of the ball and try to keep them there through the impact before releasing them naturally at the last possible moment. If you flip the wrists the likely result will be a short duff or a skulled shot across the green.

Tip 18: Read chips like you read putts

If you want to chip the ball close you need to read the green like you do your putts. Most people just chip towards the flag without really thinking of where to land the ball, how far it will run, or in what direction. You should pick a target point where you want to land the ball (allowing for the roll) and chip to that mark. It should improve your touch significantly.

Tip 19: Hitting out of sand with confidence

Many amateurs don't perform well out of sand and in many cases this stems from a lack of confidence. On every other type of golf shot players take a practice swing before they hit the ball which builds muscle memory and increases confidence. However you can't do this in a bunker because it is illegal to ground your club and make a practice swing. To get around this try a practice shot by the side of the bunker, then walk confidently up to the ball and repeat it in the sand.

Tip 20: Use different clubs but the same swing for different length chips

A lot of players have a favourite club for chipping (usually a wedge), so when they are faced with different length chips they often use the same club and vary their swing speed. An alternative method to encourage consistency is to use the same swing on all chips but vary the club for different distances. It all depends on how much green you have to work with because ideally you want to get the ball on the ground and moving as early as possible. You need to learn how much roll each club produces so that you can aim to land your chip the right distance away from the flag. Longer clubs with lower loft will roll further, whereas higher lofted clubs will stop more quickly but allow you to fly the ball over obstacles. To give you an indication, a wedge will typically cover about 50% of the distance in the air and 50% on the ground, whereas a seven iron will cover 25% in the air and 75% on the ground.

Tip 21: Hitting out of sand

Common problems for amateurs are hitting down and decelerating. You need to have a fairly explosive swing to get out of sand; if you decelerate you will find the ball about five inches in front of where you just played it. Believe that a full swing will still result in a short shot because you are actually striking the sand behind the ball, not the ball itself. For fluffy sand aim to hit about an inch behind the ball; for wet sand half that distance and shorten the swing. The less sand you take the faster the ball will come out. Make sure you sweep through the ball rather than hitting down, and ensure that the fastest point of the swing is about six inches behind the ball.

Putting

When I was a beginner I didn't find putting very exciting; instead I wanted to devote all my energy into figuring out how to hit 300 yard plus drives like my friends. However avoiding 3 putts can make a substantial impact on your score, so take on board the following tips as a really simple way to achieve that.

Tip 22: Hitting long putts

Being able to lag the long putts close is the key to not three putting. To make it easier don't focus on the hole; imagine a bigger area to hit into such as a dustbin lid. Try and roll the ball into that lid and you should always be in tap in range.

Tip 23: Keep your head still

When you take your putting stroke make sure that you keep your head absolutely still throughout. There is a temptation to watch the putter swinging back or through to check that you are online, and a further temptation to look up and watch the ball to the hole. Both can cause involuntary body movements that will stop you making a pure stroke on the putt. This is a hard discipline to master and it will feel odd to change from what you do now. Your distance control may suffer while you get used to this, but please persevere and trust that this is the key to better putting.

Tip 24: Hitting breaking putts

With breaking putts there is a tendency not to trust that the ball will turn; consequently the player "steers" the putt by turning the putter face and the ball ends up missing. It is hard to visualise a breaking putt; you actually need to focus on hitting a straight putt and stop thinking about the hole altogether, that way your technique is less likely to breakdown. Instead, pick a point on the green where you believe the putt will break. Hit the ball to that point and gravity will take care of the rest.

Tip 25: Getting a feel for downhill putts.

It is often difficult to get a feel for how hard you should hit a downhill putt so that it doesn't run way past the hole. As with the previous tip visualising a different target can often help. For example if the hole is twenty feet away and downhill, you could pick a point on the green which is fifteen feet away and pretend the hole is there. Hit the putt as hard as you would if the imaginary hole was on a flat green. This will give you a good feel for hitting a softer putt and the slope of the green will accelerate the ball so it rolls the extra five feet to the hole. Obviously you will need to experiment with this but the steeper the slope the closer you should move the imaginary hole towards you.

Tip 26: No peeking on putting

Every amateur's worst mistake when putting is watching to see if the ball has gone in the hole instead of concentrating on hitting the putter straight down the target line. If you look up you will inevitably compromise your contact with the ball. Tall players especially suffer because they have a tendency to lift up and hit the ball thin. This costs the player a clean contact and solid distance control. If you hit putts short and the ball doesn't seem to come off the putter face very well, that may be why. It takes a lot of discipline not to look so try closing your left eye when you putt so you can't see the target in your peripheral vision.

Tip 27: Miss like a pro

Have you ever watched a player on television miss one of those hard breaking putts and heard the commentators talk about him missing on the pro side of the hole? On a breaking putt it is considered "more professional" to miss the putt above the hole by giving it too much power than to miss below the hole when you haven't given it enough. There is actually a scientific reason why it is better to miss above the hole. On the pro side the ball is moving towards the hole as it runs out whereas on the amateur side the ball is moving away. This means a putt on the amateur side is less likely to go in, and if you do miss, your return putt could be longer.

Tip 28: Use the ball to aim up your putts

If you have ever watched professionals on the driving range before a tournament you may have noticed them drawing black lines on their balls using a marker pen. You see the reason why on the first green when they mark and clean their ball before replacing it so that the line on the ball is aiming at the hole. They then use this line to help them line up the putt. This is something the amateur golfer should copy! Often you won't need to use a marker pen because there will be some writing, a line, or a logo you can use instead. If all of this sounds like a lot of bother for little return, bear in mind that it is extremely difficult to aim when you are stood directly above the ball looking down. If professionals feel like they need a little extra help in alignment you will be even further off. You only need to be a few degrees out in judgement to cause a miss even if you hit the ball perfectly. Taking the time to align the ball removes this visual guess work and will improve your putting accuracy.

Tip 29: Controlling downhill putts

When hitting a short downhill putt it is very easy to hit the ball too hard without meaning to. Just making a legal stroke (rather than a push) means you have to put a certain amount of force on the ball; this makes it hard to hit the ball gently enough. My tip is to hit the ball out of the toe of the putter face rather than the sweet spot in the middle; this should make the putt feel softer and allow it to come off the face more gently.

Tip 30: Long putts

On every putt you have to focus on two things; direction and speed. With long putts you shouldn't worry too much about reading the line, instead you need to focus almost entirely on speed. It's no good being online if you are ten feet long or short, but it is OK to be a foot or two left or right if you are hole high. You still have a tap in.

Tip 31: Putts flow like water

If you are struggling to read which way the green slopes, try imagining which way water would run if you poured some onto the green. This visual image should help you "see" the line of your putt. Also remember if there is a water source like a pond or river putts will tend to break towards it.

Course Management

Course management is about making good decisions so that you don't get yourself into trouble. However recognising that the average beginner will spend most of their time in trouble anyway I have devoted some tips to help you get out of tricky spots.

Tip 32: Playing into the wind

To beat the wind take an extra club than you would do normally from that distance and concentrate on swinging smoothly. If you try to hit your normal club harder you will create more backspin, which combined with the head wind will create more lift. This will result in a shot that seems to fizz off your clubface, climbs up high, and then hangs in the air before dropping straight down thirty yards short of where you had hoped. Swinging slowly with a longer club will create a lower, more penetrating ball flight, and generate less distance sapping backspin.

Tip 33: Hitting out of trees

If you end up somewhere you don't want to be like in a group of trees learn to take your medicine. Play out of the big gap even if that means going sideways or even backwards. Too many players go for a tiny space or just hit and hope. Ignore your friends who tell you that trees are ninety percent air. The practice net near the first tee is ninety five percent air, but the ball won't go through that either!

Tip 34: Hitting out of trees (part 2)

How many times have you tried to hit through a gap between two tree trunks only to plough the ball straight into one of them? If you were deliberately aiming at that tree you couldn't hit it if your life depended on it, so why when you want to avoid it does the ball seem inevitably drawn in that direction? Ironically you can avoid playing tree trunk pinball by deliberately aiming at one of the trees. Aim at the right hand of the two trees and then deliberately pull your shot slightly, you will find it a far more reliable way of making it through the gap.

Tip 35: Playing when the ground is very wet

It's all too easy to hit the ball "fat" when the ground is very wet and soft. Firstly players who get away with a swing that is too steep in the dry wont get away with it in the wet because the club will dig into the ground before it hits the ball. Secondly there is a temptation to try and muscle up on the club knowing that the ball won't roll as far when it lands, which encourages a poorer swing. To overcome the wet you should take an extra club than normal for that distance (as if you are playing into the wind) to allow for the reduced roll. Concentrate on making a wide takeaway low to the ground and then swing smoothly and in tempo. That way you are more likely to sweep the ball off the ground rather than coming down too steeply. The same principle of a wide and low takeaway applies to chip shots in the wet as well.

Tip 36: Hitting out of the rough

To hit out of the rough you should play the ball further back in your stance to promote a more solid strike. Open the clubface at address before you grip the club because the grass will close the face through impact de-lofting the club and preventing the ball getting into the air. The thicker the rough the more it will close the clubface.

Tip 37: Hitting out of the rough in the wet

To very new amateurs hitting out of short rough is easier than hitting off the tightly cut grass of the fairway, especially if the ball is sat up nicely on a tuft of grass just like a tee. I spent a lot of my early rounds hitting from these lies. Just beware that when it is wet you can actually catch water droplets between the clubface and the ball causing what is known as a "flyer". The ball can travel ten yards further than you expected so factor this into your club selection.

Tip 38: Don't aim negatively

Don't focus on where you don't want the ball to go or you may find that your mind subconsciously sends the ball there anyway. When you take aim you should avoid thoughts such as "don't hit that bunker", "or that water hazard", "or those trees". This is negative aiming and promotes the hazard in your mind. Instead you should ignore the hazard and aim at the point on the fairway or green where you <u>do</u> want the ball to go.

Tip 39: Shot selection

Making a decision about what golf shot to take is a little bit like gambling in a casino. Occasionally you will get lucky and win some money, but over time the house always wins. On the course you can select safe shots or risky shots; but if you want your scoring to be consistent you should always take the safe option. You might pull off that miracle shot between two trees, but most of the time you won't, and it will cost you extra shots that you didn't need to waste. If you think you could pull of a shot successfully less than seven times out of ten then don't take it!

Tip 40: Hitting from poor lies

Generally speaking if you have a bad lie you should play the ball slightly further back in your stance. It will help promote a cleaner contact meaning you are less likely to miss hit.

Tip 41: Hitting a mud ball

When you are faced with a ball which has a chunk of mud on it you need to know how that will affect the ball's behaviour in the air. Generally speaking the ball will curve the opposite direction to the side of the ball the mud is on. Adjust your aim to account for this and then play the shot as you would do if you were playing into a headwind. Take an extra club and use a smooth, slower swing which will produce less backspin. Don't hit the ball hard because the added backspin will accentuate the un-stability of the ball sending it shooting off in an unpredictable direction.

Tip 42: Never aim into trouble

A lot of people take into account their natural shot shape when aiming; for example somebody who plays a ten yard fade might aim ten yards left of the green hoping that the fade of the ball will bring the ball back online. This is a good approach as long as you obey one rule; never aim into trouble assuming that your shot shape will bring the ball back into safety. What if you hit it straight? You never want to be punished for hitting a good shot.

Tip 43: Ball below or above your feet

If the ball is above your feet you need to choke down the club. If you try and hold it normally you will have to lean way back to make contact with the ball. You will be amazed how little distance you lose choking down the handle of the club. Doing this allows your swing mechanics to stay the same while still picking the ball neatly off the ground. If the ball is below your feet it is more tricky. You need to bend your legs to get down to the ball, while trying to keep your back and other swing mechanics the same as a regular shot. Your one swing thought should be "stay down" as you hit the shot. If your head and body come up you will hit it thin. Whether the ball is above or below your feet swing easy and don't try too hard, or your tight muscles will tend to bring the club up causing a thin contact.

Mental Game

Golf is a game played as much in your head as physically out on the course. When you are new to the game you have low expectations so you don't need to worry too much, but as you get better and threaten to beat your personal bests you will experience pressure. The following tips will help you to cope with the ups and downs you will inevitably encounter during a round.

Tip 44: Freezing over the ball or too much tension

Some golfers become obsessed with set up and grip to the point where they don't feel comfortable over the ball or ready to hit. Negative thoughts enter the head and desperate to escape the stress the golfer lashes at the ball. More often than not the result ends up being a disaster. To remove the tension many players incorporate a trigger to begin the swing process. A good one is to slightly press your hands forward ahead of the clubface before starting the back swing. This works on putts as well.

Tip 45: Controlling your emotions

I've lost count of the number of times I've put together a run of great holes, become over-excited about what I might shoot, only to implode under the pressure and shoot a horrible number. You should never think about the whole round in its entirety or try to project what you might score. Play each hole as a separate unrelated event and try to keep your emotional reaction the same whether you make a bogey or a birdie.

Tip 46: Getting used to handling pressure

It is very easy to nonchalantly bang in 3 feets putts on the practice green without a problem. But out on the course when faced with the same three feet putt for par, how many amateurs miss because of a shaky stroke? The only difference between these two scenarios is the existence of pressure. To get used to handling pressure out on the course you need to add an element of it into your practice sessions. Try placing a bet with a playing partner to introduce a competition environment; whoever misses the putt has to give their ball away to the other player. You will be amazed how different that putt now feels (especially if you play with expensive new balls).

Tip 47: Know when to back off a shot

How many times have you gone through your pre shot routine and addressed the ball, only to feel uncomfortable, or be distracted by something at the point of starting your swing? You know you should stop but you carry on anyway telling yourself it's too late now or it will be okay. The resulting duff sends the ball twenty yards up the fairway slightly short of where your divot has landed. If you do find yourself distracted as you begin your swing make sure you have the discipline to back off the shot and go through your pre shot routine again. Don't worry about holding up your playing partners; it will still be quicker than looking for your ball in the trees and preferable to the embarrassment of taking your second shot from just off the front of the tee box!

Tip 48: Clear your mind

You have been playing well, but a sloppy error caused you to make a bad score on the last hole. You are furious with yourself, and you take that anger with you onto the tee box of the next hole. Your mind is not fully focused on the shot because you are still dwelling on the past and before you know it you have turned one bad hole into two. You spiral down until you realise that you have let one bad shot derail your entire round. Does this scenario sound familiar? It is okay to get angry about making a mistake but you must clear your negative emotions before you take your next shot. To help you to do this try drawing an imaginary line in the fairway ahead of you. As you walk towards it permit yourself to think about the mistake and beat yourself up, but, as soon as you cross that line you must let it go and focus only on the next shot. This visualisation technique can help you stay in the present where you need to be.

Tip 49: Don't rush when on another fairway

Everyone hits a wild tee shot now and then and ends up on the fairway of another hole facing the humiliation of playing their recovery shot while the people actually playing that hole have to stop and wait. It is embarrassing, and is made even more so when we rush the shot in an attempt to get out of the way and make a complete mess of it. If you are one of the many people who feel uncomfortable in this situation stop and ask yourself how you would feel with the roles reversed. Would you mind waiting two minutes while someone else plays a shot from your fairway? Most people will say no. Armed with the knowledge that most players don't mind; play the shot properly and don't rush it.

Tip 50: Keep stats to target game improvement

If you have limited time to practice you need to make sure the practice sessions you do have are effective. However most people don't realise which elements of their game need to improve. To resolve this I recommend conducting an analysis of your game by keeping statistics of your next three rounds. How many fairways were hit, how many greens in regulation, how often did you get down in three from inside 100 yards, how many putts did you take, and how many times did you three putt? You might be very surprised where you lose shots. To illustrate this point consider the following experience of one of my friends. My friend who played off a handicap of 21 was convinced he needed to work on his tee shots to lower his score because he always teed off with a 5 iron and couldn't hit woods. One day he played with a senior golfer, who despite being a short hitter, played off single figures. My friend found that his 5 iron drive was not far away from the distance the older player hit his driver; therefore after one shot they were in the same place on the fairway. However, from 100 yards in the older player was far superior and finished fifteen shots better over eighteen holes. Only when he was faced with that example did my friend realise he needed to practice approach shots from 100 yards in, and chips from the side of the green, the two areas he was weaker in.

Tip 51: Mix it up

If you tend to play the same course you have probably found that you make the same mistakes on the same hole over and over again. For example I always used to double bogey the third hole because I always sliced my drive into the trees on the right. My friends suggested that I hit an iron short of the trees to ensure I made the fairway albeit slightly further back. My average for that hole is now much better. Good course management should take into account all the information you have, so don't mindlessly keep playing the same hole in the same unsuccessful way.

Tip 52: Getting your head right for competition

Entering a competition or club medal adds additional pressure to what you may have experienced previously playing with your friends. Because of this it can be a mistake to take the competition too seriously. When I entered a medal I used to start with a brand new ball, maybe a new glove, I would clean my clubs, and take extra practice before the round. By the time I hit my first tee shot I had worked myself up so much that the first few holes were a disaster. What I really needed was to feel comfortable, and the best way to do that is through familiarity of routine. That's why I believe you should approach a medal as if you are just playing with your friends. One other thing; aiming to shoot a really low round rarely works, so just play and see what happens.

Tip 53: Play your own game

Never get caught up in club vanity and never try to match the club selection of your playing partner. There is an unspoken macho element to golf which tends to have an unwanted influence on your scoring. Let's be honest, we all want to out hit our friends because it signifies that we are either stronger or better than them. Believe me getting caught up in this will only have a negative effect on your score. Choose your club as if you were out on the course by yourself. I struggled with this for a long time because I had to learn to swallow my pride. When I started I was around 3 stone heavier and 3 inches taller than my playing partners, so naturally I felt that I should be able to out hit them. This was never the case and the harder I tried the worse the results. To illustrate how technique is more important than strength, I have watched my 5 feet 10 inch, 11 stone friend hit 350 yard drives that I have failed to get past in two shots!

Common Mistakes

The final section is devoted to common mistakes that I believe all new players will make at some point. Golf is a game of opposites and some of the technically correct things we are told to do make no logical sense at all. For that reason you are unlikely to stumble upon the correct methods by chance; so it's better if somebody takes the time to tell you! I've wasted many rounds of golf making the mistakes below so that you don't have to. When you read below you may smile to yourself knowingly, thinking yeah I do that. So I ask you, if you know you are doing it wrong, why do you keep doing it? It seems that every golfer is cursed with a dose of insanity. The definition of which is, doing the same thing over and over again and expecting a different outcome. Hopefully having someone else highlight these examples of insanity to you will encourage you to see the error of your ways.

Tip 54: Get your clubs custom fitted

One of the most important things a new player can do is get their clubs custom fitted. When asked, Tiger Woods ranked this as the most important advice he would give a beginner. If you are serious about getting better this is crucial! If the clubs are the wrong size you will be forced to make compensations in your setup and swing which will hold you back. Ninety percent of the people who read this tip will dismiss it; be warned, don't.

Tip 55: Stop tinkering

The ultimate goal for a player is to develop a consistent and repeatable swing that stands up under pressure. You can only achieve this through repetition. Most amateurs either, take lessons, take tips from magazines, or copy tips from more experienced friends. They are constantly tinkering with their swing and trying something new, this means each time they go out and play they are effectively using a brand new and unpractised swing. Many amateurs actually get worse after taking lessons because they move away from what's natural. If you want to improve you should get some advice up to a point, but then stick with it and work on grooving it.

Tip 56: Swing smoothly

Any player can improve dramatically if they introduce a bit of discipline into their swing and reduce their ego. Why are we so concerned about out-hitting our playing partners or hitting it as far as the pros? While you think about that, here is the reason why it is a bad idea. Trying to swing hard creates tension which means the sequencing of the swing can be thrown out to the point where the club head is actually slowing down at impact rather than accelerating. The golf swing should be smooth; a good analogy here is swinging a rope. If you yank a rope instead of pulling it smoothly the end snatches and slows down, the only way to accelerate the end of the rope is to pull smoothly; it's the same with your club face.

Tip 57: Don't allow the range to discourage you

When you practice on the range don't read too much into how far you are hitting the ball. Most ranges use low compression balls which fly ten percent shorter than the balls you use on the course. The yardage markers on the range are often inaccurate too so don't over swing; just focus on grooving a good swing and a solid shot shape.

Tip 58: Grip Pressure

Gripping the club too tightly can cause any number of problems. Let's begin with the putter. Do you ever feel like you can't lag long putts, can't get the speed right on short breaking putts, or find yourself steering the ball with the club face? If the answer is yes the chances are you're gripping too tightly. Grip pressure can cause you problems with the irons and woods too; if you grip too tightly you will impede club head release which can cost you accuracy and distance. To find the right grip pressure imagine a scale of one to ten where one is so light the club almost drops from your hands and ten is where it would be impossible for someone to pull the club out of your hands. Ideally you should aim for a grip pressure of between four and five with the putter and five and six on the irons.

Tip 59: Hip slide kills distance

Many amateurs attempting to hit the ball harder end up suffering from hip slide. This is where the hips slide to the right instead of the shoulders and hips turning as they should. To avoid hip slide make sure your hips don't move outside your right knee on the backswing; you should feel some pressure on the inside of your right knee as you resist. It will feel unnatural to begin with but actually produces more power and a cleaner strike.

Tip 60: Shorten your backswing for better ball striking

Shortening your backswing can often lead to better ball striking; and because of this extra distance too. While a longer backswing in theory gives you more power the trade off in lost control means it's not worth it. The last 10% of the backswing might give you an extra 10% in power but you probably sacrifice double that in control. There is less to go wrong on a shorter backswing, especially as most amateurs get to parallel at the top by cupping their wrists rather than turning their body, which leads to a "handsy" swing. To be a purer striker of the ball, swing to what you believe is about 60%; in reality you will swinging closer to 80%, which is about perfect.

Tip 61: Warming up isn't for wimps

The golf swing is such a finely calibrated mechanism that it doesn't take much to throw it out of sync and cause some disastrous shots. If your muscles are stiff you won't be able to swing freely and your swing mechanics will be out. Most people don't bother warming up properly before a round; instead they loosen up during their first few holes. Why risk shooting a bad score early on and waste unnecessary shots? Make sure you are stretched, warmed up and your swing is grooved, otherwise you will waste the first few holes sorting it out. Sound like common sense? Then why don't you do it?

Tip 62: To get a score, play with what you've got

When you enter a medal or a club competition you need to shoot a good score on that given day. For this reason you should always play with the swing you turn up with rather than trying to fix it. For example if you find you are hitting a bit of a fade on that day, work with it and adjust your aim to compensate. Don't try and change your swing plane to fix the swing problems during a competition round. You will find that you get a better score more often.

Tip 63: Paralysis by analysis

There are so many things to think about during a golf swing; which is why you shouldn't think about any of them! From start to finish there are literally hundreds of checkpoints to tick off in the perfect swing. If you look at an instructional book there are hundreds of pages showing you what position each part of your body should be at each stage of the swing. It would be nice to consciously check off all these points as you swing, but unfortunately the full golf swing can take as little as a second to complete. It just isn't possible to process all that information in that time frame which is why the swing must be an unconscious event relying on muscle memory only. Most amateurs are trying to process too many swing thoughts and this conscious effort is preventing them swinging smoothly. At the very most you should have one swing thought, any more and your brain can't cope.

Tip 64: Why does the club twist in my hands?

If the club twists in your hands when you hit a shot, it's probably because you are hitting the ball off the toe (end) of the clubface. Many beginners mistakenly believe that they just need to grip the club harder, but it doesn't matter how hard you grip, if you hit the ball out of the toe the club will twist. The only prevention is to hit the ball out of the middle. There are many reasons why you can't "reach" the ball, but the simplest could be standing too far away from it at address.

Tip 65: Am I hitting the sweet spot?

Each clubface has a sweet spot; the point in the middle of the club where the club works best when it impacts the ball. You need to strike here to get the best distance and consistent ball flight. Analysing where you hit the ball can help you modify your setup so that you hit the sweet spot more often. To do this take a ball and draw a dot on the back of it with a marker pen. When you hit the ball it should leave a pen mark on the clubface indicating exactly where on the club you hit the ball. Try a few swings and then adjust your set up to centralise the impact point.

Tip 66: Improve your fitness for lower scoring

Have you ever started a round really well only to fade over the last few holes by making a few sloppy mistakes? It's probably because you aren't fit enough. An average eighteen hole course is nearly four miles long and takes four hours to play. That can be fairly demanding and even a slight amount of tiredness or stiffness is enough to throw off the golf swing. You don't want to compromise your score because your body cannot cope so make the effort to improve your golf fitness through resistance training, cardio, and stretching.

Tip 67: Be realistic on club selection

A good golfer relies on experience; memories of what you did in similar situations will help you make good decisions in the present. However your memory needs to be accurate rather than rose tinted. For example when choosing your club selection to hit a 200 yard shot into the green you need to think how well your average shot from that distance has been. Don't remember the one 7 iron you hit 200 yards down wind, downhill, on hard ground last summer. Think about the carry and what you can reliably hit. Play to your average, not to your personal best.

Tip 68: Make practice realistic

When you practice on the driving range, try not to just blast through 50 balls in ten minutes flat and then go home thinking you are great. Practice only makes perfect if it is quality practice. On each shot go through the same pre shot routine that you would if you were stood on the tee during a round. To work on your alignment make sure you aim at a target. Pick a flag on the driving range and pretend it is the flag on a green. Don't just mindlessly hit balls out into a field, that won't improve your ball striking or accuracy.

Tip 69: Keep the same ball

If you want to develop consistent range control on everything from your approach shots to chips on the green then you need to use the same ball. There are many different brands with different features, hard and soft, extra spin, high launch etc. Some balls may be ten or twenty yards longer than others while some will roll more than others on the green. You can't develop feel if each ball you use reacts differently each time because you are using ones you found in the long grass, or the ones that were on offer.

Tip 70: Practice Pitching on the Range

Most people only practice full shots on the range, but your approach shots from one hundred yards in are much more significant for your score. Most people don't feel that comfortable hitting less than full shots into the green because they haven't practiced them. Mastering that will take more shots off your handicap than practicing a nice looking tee shot.

Tip 71: When in doubt, club up

When you have a shot into the green and you are between clubs, should you take the shorter club and try and muscle up on it, or, take the longer club and swing easy? The answer is obvious; you are more likely to be on target with a smooth swing, but 90% of people will choose to muscle up instead. More often than not you sacrifice proper mechanics meaning an off line shot, or ironically a shorter shot than normal with that club because of a poor strike.

Tip 72: Golf is about opposites, hit down to get the ball up

This tip will help every shot from chipping to the full swing. Most people think they need to hit upwards to get the ball in the air. Instead you should hit down because the golf clubface is designed to contact the ball on the downswing, not the upswing (the only exception being the long woods). You need to trap the ball between the ground and the clubface which compresses it, the ball will then decompress and move up the clubface inheriting backspin and the energy required to shoot it up into the air. Now you understand how it works focus on hitting down on the ball instead of trying to flip it up.

###

Printed in Great Britain
by Amazon